The CHILD Mass book

The Complete Order of Mass
together with the
Three Eucharistic Prayers for Children

Text approved by the
Bishops' Committee on the Liturgy

THE REGINA PRESS
NEW YORK

The Order of Mass

Introductory Rites

We come to Mass together to praise and thank God for all that he has done for us.

Entrance Song

As the priest comes in we sing an entrance song or if there is no singing we say the special antiphon for that day.

Greeting

Priest In the name of the Father, and of the Son, and of the Holy Spirit.

All **Amen.**

Priest The grace of our Lord Jesus Christ and the love of God and the fellowship of the Holy Spirit be with you all.

People **And also with you.**

One of the following greetings may be used instead of the above. He then may introduce the Mass with a few words.

Priest The grace and peace of God our Father and the Lord Jesus Christ be with you.

People **Blessed be God, the Father of our Lord Jesus Christ.**

or

People And also with you.

or

Priest The Lord be with you.

People **And also with you.**

3

Penitential Rite

The Priest asks us to think of how we have failed to be the loving people God wants us to be and to tell God we are sorry.

Priest   My brothers and sisters,
to prepare ourselves to celebrate the sacred mysteries
let us call to mind our sins.
Silence.

All   **I confess to almighty God,**
and to you, my brothers and sisters,
that I have sinned through my own fault
(all strike their breast)
in my thoughts and in my words,
in what I have done,
and in what I have failed to do;
and I ask blessed Mary, ever virgin,
all the angels and saints,
and you, my brothers and sisters,
to pray for me to the Lord our God.

Instead of these words the priest might use one of the following acts of sorrow, or similar prayers.

Priest   Lord, we have sinned against you:
Lord, have mércy.
People   **Lord, have mercy.**
Priest   Lord, show us your mercy and love.
People   **And grant us your salvation.**

4

or

Priest	You were sent to heal the contrite:
	Lord, have mercy.
People	**Lord, have mercy.**
Priest	You came to call sinners:
	Christ, have mercy.
People	**Christ, have mercy.**
Priest	You plead for us at the right hand of the Father:
	Lord, have mercy.
People	**Lord, have mercy.**

At the end of any of the acts of sorrow the priest says:

Priest	May almighty God have mercy on us,
	forgive us our sins,
	and bring us to everlasting life.
People	**Amen.**

Kyrie

Priest	Lord, have mercy.
People	**Lord, have mercy.**
Priest	Christ, have mercy.
People	**Christ, have mercy.**
Priest	Lord, have mercy.
People	**Lord, have mercy.**

5

Gloria

This song of praise is sung or said by all on big feasts and all Sundays except in Lent and Advent

All **Glory to God in the highest,
and peace to his people on earth.**

**Lord God, heavenly King,
almighty God and Father,
we worship you, we give you thanks,
we praise you for your glory.**

**Lord Jesus Christ, only Son of the Father,
Lord God, Lamb of God,
you take away the sin of the world:
have mercy on us;
you are seated at the right hand of the Father:
receive our prayer.**

**For you alone are the Holy One,
you alone are the Lord,
you alone are the Most High,
Jesus Christ,
with the Holy Spirit,
in the glory of God the Father. Amen.**

Opening Prayer

Priest Let us pray.

We stand and pray silently for a while before the priest reads the special prayer for the day. At the end of the prayer we answer:

All **Amen.**

The Liturgy of the Word

On Sundays there are three readings from the Sacred Scriptures. Through these readings God's Word is given to us through the Church. The most solemn reading is taken from one of the Gospels and we all stand as we hear what Jesus said and did.

First reading

At the end of the reading:

Reader   This is the Word of the Lord.

All   **Thanks be to God.**

Responsorial Psalm

We repeat the response said by the reader the first time and then after each verse.

Second Reading

At the end of the reading:

Reader   This is the Word of the Lord.

All   **Thanks be to God.**

Gospel Acclamation

We stand and sing or say a verse of welcome.

Gospel Reading

Priest   The Lord be with you.
People **And also with you.**
Priest   A reading from the holy gospel according to N.
People **Glory to you, Lord.**

At the end of the Gospel we say:
All **Praise to you, Lord Jesus Christ.**

Homily

The priest explains the Word of God and teaches us.

Profession of Faith

We express our belief in God

We believe in one God,
   the Father, the Almighty,
   maker of heaven and earth,
   of all that is seen and unseen.

We believe in one Lord, Jesus Christ,
   the only Son of God,
   eternally begotten of the Father,
   God from God, Light from Light,
   true God from true God,
   begotten, not made, one in Being with the Father.
   Through him all things were made.
   For us men and for our salavation
      he came down from heaven: All bow
by the power of the Holy Spirit
   he was born of the Virgin Mary, and
      became man.

For our sake he was crucified under Pontius Pilate;
   he suffered, died and was buried.
   On the third day he rose again
      in fulfillment of the Scriptures;
   he ascended into heaven
      and is seated at the right hand of the Father.
He will come again in glory to judge the living and
   the dead, and his kingdom will have no end.

We believe in the Holy Spirit, the Lord, the giver of
    life,
  who proceeds from the Father and the Son.
  With the Father and the Son he is worshiped and
    glorified.
  He has spoken through the Prophets.
  We believe in one holy catholic and apostolic
    Church.
  We acknowledge one baptism for the forgiveness
    of sins.
  We look for the resurrection of the dead,
    and the life of the world to come. Amen.

The General Intercessions

After the Profession of Faith the priest begins the General
Intercessions the special prayer asking for the needs of all
the people. After the priest says the introduction, the
petitions are offered by the deacon or a member of the
assembly, we respond, after each petition, to show that we
join with the priest. The priest says a final prayer and we all
reply:

All **Amen.**

Liturgy of the Eucharist

We bring gifts of bread and wine. The priest puts wine and a little water into the chalice and puts it on the altar near the bread. The bread and wine are our gifts which are going to become the body and blood of Jesus. They are put on the altar because it is God's table. On it, the gifts offered to him are placed; from it, he gives us the sacred banquet.

Our gifts are brought to the priest while the altar is being prepared. A song may now be sung.

Before placing the bread on the altar, the priest says:

Priest **Blessed are you, Lord, God of all creation.**
Through your goodness we have this bread to offer,
which earth has given and human hands have made.
It will become for us the bread of life.

12

If there is no singing we respond:

People **Blessed be God for ever.**

Before placing the chalice on the altar, the priest says:

Priest Blessed are you, Lord, God of all creation.
Through your goodness we have this wine to offer,
fruit of the vine and work of human hands.
It will become our spiritual drink.

If there is no singing we respond:

People **Blessed be God for ever.**

Invitation to Prayer

The priest washes his hands and invites us to pray with him.

Priest Pray, brethren, that our sacrifice
may be acceptable to God, the almighty Father.
People **May the Lord accept the sacrifice at your
hands
for the praise and glory of his name,
for our good, and the good of all his Church.**

Prayer over the gifts.

The priest then says the special prayer for the day.
At the end we say: **Amen.**

THE EUCHARISTIC PRAYER

There is a choice of four Eucharistic Prayers and all express our offering of sacrifice in adoration and thanksgiving and pray for the needs of all God's people, living and dead. In addition there are three special prayers for Masses with young people which you will find on page 43. At each Mass only one Eucharistic Prayer is said.

Dialogue

Priest   The Lord be with you.
People   **And also with you.**
Priest   Lift up your hearts.
People   **We lift them up to the Lord.**
Priest   Let us give thanks to the Lord our God.
People   **It is right to give him thanks and praise.**

Preface

The priest says or sings the preface. There are numerous prefaces for different occasions; but all are prayers of praise and thanksgiving. At the end we all join in:

Sanctus

All   **Holy, holy, holy Lord, God of power and might, heaven and earth are full of your glory.**
     Hosanna in the highest.
Blessed is he who comes in the name of the Lord.
     Hosanna in the highest.

Eucharistic Prayer I

The priest may decide not to say the parts in brackets.

We praise God and ask him to accept our offering.

We come to you, Father,
with praise and thanksgiving,
through Jesus Christ your Son.
Through him we ask you to accept and bless
these gifts we offer you in sacrifice.

We pray for the Church

We offer them for your holy catholic Church,
watch over it, Lord, and guide it;
grant it peace and unity throughout the world.
We offer them for N. our Pope,
for N. our bishop,
and for all who hold and teach the catholic faith
that comes to us from the apostles.

We pray for those here today

Remember, Lord, your people,
especially those for whom we now pray, N. and N.
Remember all of us gathered here before you.
You know how firmly we believe in you
and dedicate ourselves to you.
We offer you this sacrifice of praise
for ourselves and those who are dear to us.
We pray to you, our living and true God,
for our well-being and redemption.

We honor Mary and the Saints.

In union with the whole Church
we honor Mary,
the ever-virgin mother of Jesus Christ our Lord
    and God.
We honor Joseph, her husband,
the apostles and martyrs
Peter and Paul, Andrew,
(James, John, Thomas,
James, Philip,
Bartholemew, Matthew, Simon and Jude;
we honor Linus, Cletus, Clement, Sixtus,
Cornelius, Cyprian, Lawrence, Chrysogonus,
John and Paul, Cosmas and Damian)
and all the saints.
May their merits and prayers
gain us your constant help and protection.
(Through Christ our Lord. Amen.)

We ask God to accept our offering

Father, accept this offering
from your whole family.
Grant us your peace in this life,
save us from final damnation,
and count us among those you have chosen.
(Through Christ our Lord. Amen)

Bless and approve our offering;
make it acceptable to you,
an offering in spirit and in truth.

Let it become for us
the body and blood of Jesus Christ,
your only Son, our Lord.

Our offering becomes the Body and Blood of Christ

The day before he suffered
he took bread in his sacred hands
and looking up to heaven,
to you, his almighty Father,
he gave you thanks and praise.
He broke the bread,
gave it to his disciples and said:

Take this, all of you, and eat it:
this is my body which will be given up for you.

When supper was ended,
he took the cup.
Again he gave you thanks and praise,
gave the cup to his disciples, and said:

Take this, all of you, and drink from it:
this is the cup of my blood,
the blood of the new and everlasting covenant.
It will be shed for you and for all
so that sins may be forgiven.
Do this in memory of me.

The priest invites us to renew our faith in the mystery of Christ's death, resurrection and coming again.

Priest   Let us proclaim the mystery of faith:

People   1   **Christ has died,**
           Christ is risen,
           Christ will come again.

       2   **Dying you destroyed our death,**
           rising you restored our life.
           Lord Jesus, come in glory.

       3   **When we eat this bread and drink this cup,**
           we proclaim your death, Lord Jesus,
           until you come in glory.

       4   **Lord, by your cross and resurrection**
           you have set us free.
           You are the Savior of the world.

We remember Jesus' death and resurrection.

Father, we celebrate the memory of Christ, your Son.
We, your people and your ministers,
recall his passion,
his resurrection from the dead,
and his ascension into glory;
and from the many gifts you have given us
we offer to you, God of glory and majesty,
this holy and perfect sacrifice:
the bread of life
and the cup of eternal salvation.

Look with favor on these offerings
and accept them as once you accepted
the gifts of your servant Abel,
the sacrifice of Abraham, our father in faith,
and the bread and wine offered by your priest
    Melchisedech.
Almighty God,
we pray that your angel may take this sacrifice
to your altar in heaven.
Then, as we receive from this altar
the sacred body and blood of your Son,
let us be filled with every grace and blessing.
(Through Christ our Lord. Amen.)

We pray for the dead

Remember, Lord, those who have died
and have gone before us marked with the sign of faith,
especially those for whom we now pray, N. and N.

May these, and all who sleep in Christ,
find in your presence
light, happiness, and peace.
(Through Christ our Lord. Amen.)

We pray for ourselves

For ourselves, too, we ask
some share in the fellowship of your apostles and
    martyrs,
with John the Baptist, Stephen, Matthias, Barnabas,
(Ignatius, Alexander, Marcellinus, Peter,
Felicity, Perpetua, Agatha, Lucy,
Agnes, Cecilia, Anastasia)
and all the saints.

Though we are sinners,
we trust in your mercy and love.
Do not consider what we truly deserve,
but grant us your forgiveness.
Through Christ our Lord.

Through him you give us all these gifts.
You fill them with life and goodness,
you bless them and make them holy.

We give solemn praise and glory to God

Through him,
with him,
in him,
in the unity of the Holy Spirit,
all glory and honor is yours,
almighty Father,
for ever and ever.
All   **Amen.**

Eucharistic Prayer II

We ask God to let the Holy Spirit bless our gifts

Lord, you are holy indeed,
the fountain of all holiness.
Let your Spirit come upon these gifts to make them
    holy,
so that they may become for us
the body and blood of our Lord, Jesus Christ.

Our offering becomes the Body and Blood of Christ

Before he was given up to death,
a death he freely accepted,
he took bread and gave you thanks.
He broke the bread,
gave it to his disciples, and said:

Take this, all of you, and eat it:
this is my body which will be given up for you.

When supper was ended, he took the cup,
Again he gave you thanks and praise,
gave the cup to his disciples, and said:

Take this, all of you, and drink from it:
this is the cup of my blood,
the blood of the new and everlasting covenant.
It will be shed for you and for all
so that sins may be forgiven.
Do this in memory of me.

The priest invites you to renew our faith in the mystery of Christ's death, resurrection and coming again.

Priest   Let us proclaim the mystery of faith:

People   1   **Christ has died,**
         Christ is risen,
         Christ will come again.

      2   **Dying you destroyed our death,**
         rising you restored our life.
         Lord Jesus, come in glory.

      3   **When we eat this bread and drink this**
           cup,
         we proclaim your death, Lord Jesus,
         until you come in glory.

      4   **Lord, by your cross and resurrection**
         you have set us free.
         You are the Savior of the world.

We remember Jesus' death and resurrection

In memory of his death and resurrection,
we offer you, Father, this life-giving bread,
this saving cup.
We thank you for counting us worthy
to stand in your presence and serve you.
May all of us who share in the body and blood of
    Christ
be brought together in unity by the Holy Spirit.

We pray for the Church

Lord, remember your Church throughout the world;
make us grow in love,
together with N. our Pope,
N. our bishop, and all the clergy.

We pray for the dead

Remember our brothers and sisters
who have gone to their rest
in the hope of rising again;
bring them and all the departed
into the light of your presence.

We pray with the Saints

Have mercy on us all;
make us worthy to share eternal life
with Mary, the virgin Mother of God,
with the apostles, and with all the saints
who have done your will throughout the ages.
May we praise you in union with them,
and give you glory
through your Son, Jesus Christ.

We give solemn praise and glory to God

Through him,
with him,
in him,
in the unity of the Holy Spirit,
all glory and honor is yours,
almighty Father,
for ever and ever.

All **Amen.**

Eucharistic Prayer III

We praise God and ask him to accept our offering

Father, you are holy indeed,
and all creation rightly gives you praise.
All life, all holiness comes from you
through your Son, Jesus Christ our Lord,
by the working of the Holy Spirit.
From age to age you gather a people to yourself,
so that from east to west
a perfect offering may be made
to the glory of your name.

We ask God to let the Holy Spirit bless our gifts

And so, Father, we bring you these gifts.
We ask you to make them holy by the power of your
   Spirit,
that they may become the body and blood
of your Son, our Lord Jesus Christ,
at whose command we celebrate this eucharist.

Our offering becomes the Body and Blood of Christ

On the night he was betrayed,
he took bread and gave you thanks and praise.
He broke the bread, gave it to his disciples, and said:

Take this, all of you, and eat it:
this is my body which will be given up for you.

When supper was ended, he took the cup.
Again he gave you thanks and praise,
gave the cup to his disciples, and said:

Take this, all of you, and drink from it:
this is the cup of my blood,
the blood of the new and everlasting covenant.
It will be shed for you and for all
so that sins may be forgiven.
Do this in memory of me.

The priest invites you to renew our faith in the mystery of Christ's death, resurrection and coming again.

Priest Let us proclaim the mystery of faith:
People 1 **Christ has died,**
             Christ is risen,
             Christ will come again.

2 **Dying you destroyed our death,**
   rising you restored our life.
   Lord Jesus, come in glory.

3 **When we eat this bread and drink this**
      cup,
   we proclaim your death, Lord Jesus,
   until you come in glory.

4 **Lord, by your cross and resurrection**
   you have set us free.
   You are the Savior of the world.

We give solemn praise and glory to God

Father, calling to mind the death your Son endured
   for our salvation,
his glorious resurrection and ascension into heaven,
and ready to greet him when he comes again,
we offer you in thanksgiving this holy and living
   sacrifice.

Look with favor on your Church's offering,
and see the Victim whose death has reconciled us to
   yourself.
Grant that we, who are nourished by his body and
   blood,
may be filled with his Holy Spirit,
and become one body, one spirit in Christ.

May he make us an everlasting gift to you
and enable us to share in the inheritance of your
   saints,
with Mary, the virgin Mother of God;
with the apostles, the martyrs,
(Saint N.—the saint of the day or patron saint) and
   all your saints,
on whose constant intercession we rely for help.

We pray for the family of God

Lord, may this sacrifice,
which has made our peace with you,
advance the peace and salvation of all the world.

Strengthen in faith and love your pilgrim Church on
    earth;
your servant, Pope N., our bishop N.,
and all the bishops,
with the clergy and the entire people your Son has
    gained for you.
Father, hear the prayers of the family you have
    gathered here before you.
In mercy and love unite all your children wherever
    they may be.

We pray for the dead

Welcome into your kingdom our departed brothers
    and sisters,
and all who have left this world in your friendship.
We hope to enjoy for ever the vision of your glory,
through Christ our Lord, from whom all good things
    come.

We give solemn praise and glory to God

Through him,
with him,
in him.
in the unity of the Holy Spirit,
all glory and honor is yours,
almighty Father,
for ever and ever.
All   **Amen.**

Eucharistic Prayer IV

Preface

Father in heaven,
it is right that we should give you thanks and glory:
you are the one God, living and true.
Through all eternity you live in unapproachable light.
Source of life and goodness, you have created all things,
to fill your creatures with every blessing
and lead all men to the joyful vision of your light.
Countless hosts of angels stand before you to do your will;
they look upon your splendor
and praise you, night and day.
United with them,
and in the name of every creature under heaven,
we too praise your glory as we say:

Sanctus

Holy, holy, holy Lord, God of power and might,
heaven and earth are full of your glory.
   Hosanna in the highest.
Blessed is he who comes in the name of the Lord.
   Hosanna in the highest.

Father, we acknowledge your greatness:
all your actions show your wisdom and love.
You formed man in your own likeness
and set him over the whole world
to serve you, his creator,
and to rule over all creatures.

Even when he disobeyed you and lost your friendship
you did not abandon him to the power of death,
but helped all men to seek and find you.
Again and again you offered a covenant to man,
and through the prophets taught him to hope for
  salvation.
Father, you so loved the world
that in the fullness of time you sent your only Son to
  be our Savior.

He was conceived through the power of the Holy
  Spirit,
and born of the Virgin Mary,
a man like us in all things but sin.
To the poor he proclaimed the good news of
  salvation,
to prisoners, freedom,
and to those in sorrow, joy.
In fulfilment of your will
he gave himself up to death;
but by rising from the dead,
he destroyed death and restored life.

And that we might live no longer for ourselves but
  for him,
he sent the Holy Spirit from you, Father,
as his first gift to those who believe,
to complete his work on earth
and bring us the fullness of grace.

Father, may this Holy Spirit sanctify these offerings.
Let them become the body and blood of Jesus Christ
  our Lord

as we celebrate the great mystery
which he left us as an everlasting covenant.

He always loved those who were his own in the world.
When the time came for him to be glorified by you,
    his heavenly Father,
he showed the depth of his love.

While they were at supper,
he took bread, said the blessing, broke the bread,
and gave it to his disciples, saying:

Take this, all of you, and eat it:
this is my body which will be given up for you.

In the same way, he took the cup, filled with wine.
He gave you thanks, and giving the cup to his
    disciples, said:

Take this, all of you, and drink from it:
this is the cup of my blood,
the blood of the new and everlasting covenant
It will be shed for you and for all
so that sins may be forgiven.
Do this in memory of me.

Priest   Let us proclaim the mystery of faith:
People   1   **Christ has died,**
               Christ is risen.
               Christ will come again.

2   **Dying you destroyed our death,
rising you restored our life.
Lord Jesus, come in glory.**

3   **When we eat this bread and drink this
cup,
we proclaim your death, Lord Jesus,
until you come in glory.**

4   **Lord, by your cross and resurrection
you have set us free.
You are the Savior of the world.**

We remember Jesus' death and resurrection

Father, we now celebrate this memorial of our
redemption.
We recall Christ's death, his descent among the dead,
his resurrection, and his ascension to your right hand;
and, looking forward to his coming in glory,
we offer you his body and blood,
the acceptable sacrifice
which brings salvation to the whole world.

We pray for God's family

Lord, look upon this sacrifice which you have given
to your Church;
and by your Holy Spirit, gather all who share this
one bread and one cup
into the body of Christ, a living sacrifice of praise.
Lord, remember those for whom we offer this sacrifice,
especially N. our Pope,
N. our bishop, and bishops and clergy everywhere.
Remember those who take part in this offering,
those here present and all your people,
and all who seek you with a sincere heart.

We pray for the dead

Remember those who have died in the peace of Christ
and all the dead whose faith is known to you alone.

We ask God to let us join the Saints in heaven

Father, in your mercy grant also to us, your children,
to enter into our heavenly inheritance
in the company of the Virgin Mary, the Mother of God,
    and your apostles and saints.
Then, in your kingdom, freed from the corruption of
    sin and death,
we shall sing your glory with every creature through
    Christ our Lord,
through whom you give us everything that is good.

We give solemn praise and glory to God

Through him,
with him,
in him,
in the unity of the Holy Spirit,
all glory and honor is yours,
almighty Father,
for ever and ever.
All **Amen.**

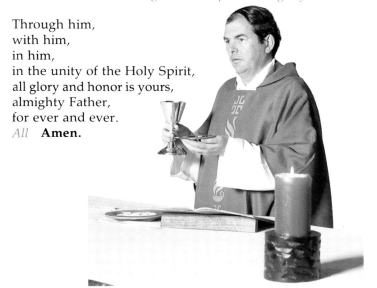

COMMUNION RITE

The Lord's Prayer

*The priest invites us to join him in saying The Lord's Prayer,
the prayer that Christ, himself, gave to his followers to say to
their Father.*

Priest   Let us pray with confidence to the Father
in the words our Savior gave us.

All   **Our Father, who art in heaven,
hallowed be thy name.
Thy kingdom come.
Thy will be done on earth, as it is in heaven.
Give us this day our daily bread,
and forgive us our trespasses,
as we forgive those who trespass against us,
and lead us not into temptation,
but deliver us from evil.**

Priest   Deliver us, Lord, from every evil,
and grant us peace in our day.
In your mercy keep us free from sin
and protect us from all anxiety
as we wait in joyful hope
for the coming of our Savior, Jesus Christ.

All   **For the kingdom, the power, and the glory are
yours, now and forever.**

Rite of Peace

The priest asks Jesus to give us the peace he promised to the apostles

Priest   Lord Jesus Christ, you said to your apostles:
I leave you peace, my peace I give you.

Look not on our sins, but on the faith of your
   Church,
and grant us the peace and unity of your kingdom
   where you live for ever and ever.   *All* **Amen.**
Priest   The peace of the Lord be with you always.
People   **And also with you.**
Priest   Let us offer each other the sign of peace.

We exchange a sign of peace and love with those near us.

The Breaking of Bread

The priest breaks the host and puts part into the chalice.
At the same time we all sing or say:

**Lamb of God, you take away the sins of the world:
   have mercy on us.
Lamb of God, you take away the sins of the world:
   have mercy on us.
Lamb of God, you take away the sins of the world:
   grant us peace.**

Communion

The priest prays quietly then lifts up the sacred host
and invites us to come to communion

Priest **This is the Lamb of God**
who takes away the sins of the world.
Happy are those who are called to his supper.
People **Lord, I am not worthy to receive you,**
but only say the word and I shall be healed.

The communion song may be sung while we receive
communion. If there is no singing the antiphon of
the day is said as we go to the altar. When giving us
communion, the priest shows us the host and says:

Priest **The body of Christ.**
People **Amen.**

After communion there may be a period of silence or a song of praise may be sung.

Prayer after Communion

We pray silently for a while before the priest reads the special prayer for the day. At the end of the prayer we say:

All   **Amen.**

Concluding Rite

It is now time for us to leave and to do good works and praise and bless the Lord in our daily lives.

Blessing

The priest blesses us in the name of Christ

Priest   The Lord be with you.
People   **And also with you.**
Priest   May almighty God bless you,
      the Father, and the Son, and the Holy Spirit.
People   **Amen.**

Sometimes on special days there is a longer blessing or a prayer over the people.

Dismissal

Priest   Go in the peace of Christ.
   or: The Mass is ended, go in peace.
   or: Go in peace to love and serve the Lord.

People   **Thanks be to God.**

GIVING AND SHARING

"Go in peace to love and serve the Lord". These are the words the priest says just before we walk out of Mass. When we do walk out is our celebration over? Do we forget about it until next week? *NO.* A very special part of our celebration is just beginning.

Mass is a time of giving and sharing. We share and celebrate as members of God's family. We give ourselves to God in our prayers and in the gifts we take up to the altar in the offertory procession. He gives himself to us in Holy Communion when we receive Christ's Body — given because he loves us and wants to help us grow more like him. We are given a final blessing and go out stronger and more able to live the Mass by giving and sharing with those around us.

Jesus knows that sometimes it is easier to be selfish and think about pleasing ourselves before others; or to hurt others by not thinking before we speak and act, about how our words and actions might make them feel. This is why he gives himself to us in Communion — to help us say "Yes — I will try as hard as I can to share His message of love".

He knows that even though we can't perform miracles as he did we can show others that we love him and want to serve him.

By sharing — our games and toys with friends or brothers and sisters.

— food, clothing and sometimes money with the poor.

By being kind and thoughtful — cheering someone up if they are sad.

— asking a lonely person to join in our games.

— doing jobs at home before being asked.

Even by giving a smile we can show others that we care about them.

It is in doing these things that we can take our Eucharistic celebration out of the Church and, with God's help, live it every day of our lives.

Eucharistic Prayers
For Masses With Children

The Eucharistic Prayer is a prayer to express our offering of sacrifice in adoration and thanksgiving. The Church has given us three special Eucharistic Prayers that may be used at Masses with children and young people.

Eucharistic Prayer for Masses with Children I

We praise and thank God for the beautiful things in our life.

Priest The Lord be with you.
People **And also with you.**
Priest Lift up your hearts.
People **We lift them up to the Lord.**
Priest Let us give thanks to the Lord our God.
People **It is right to give him thanks and praise.**
Priest God our Father,
   you have brought us here together
   so that we can give you thanks and praise
   for all the wonderful things you have done.

We thank you for all that is beautiful in the world
and for the happiness you have given us.
We praise you for daylight
and for your word which lights up our minds.
We praise you for the earth,
and all the people who live on it,
and for our life which comes from you.
We know that you are good.
You love us and do great things for us.
[So we all sing (say) together:

43

We praise God

All **Holy, holy, holy Lord, God of power and might,
heaven and earth are full of your glory.
Hosanna in the highest.]**

Priest Father,
you are always thinking about your people;
you never forget us.
You sent us your Son Jesus,
who gave his life for us
and who came to save us.
he cured sick people;
he cared for those who were poor
and wept with those who were sad.
He forgave sinners
and taught us to forgive each other.
He loved everyone
and showed us how to be kind.
He took children in his arms and blessed them.

We praise God

[So we are glad to sing (say):
All **Blessed is he who comes in the name of the Lord.
Hosanna in the highest.]**

We join the whole Church in praise

Priest God our Father,
all over the world your people praise you.

So now we pray with the whole Church:
with N., our pope and N., our bishop.
In heaven the blessed Virgin Mary,
the apostles and all the saints
always sing your praise.
Now we join with them and with the angels
to adore you as we sing (say):

We praise God

All **Holy, holy, holy Lord, God of power and might,
heaven and earth are full of your glory.
Hosanna in the highest.
Blessed is he who comes in the name of the Lord.
Hosanna in the highest.**

We ask God to send us the Holy Spirit

Priest God our Father,
you are most holy
and we want to show you that we are grateful.
We bring you bread and wine
and ask you to send your Holy Spirit to make these
gifts
the body and blood of Jesus your Son.
Then we can offer to you
what you have given to us.

Our offering becomes the Body and Blood of Christ.

On the night before he died,
Jesus was having supper with his apostles.

He took bread from the table.
He gave you thanks and praise.
Then he broke the bread, gave it to his friends,
    and said:

Take this, all of you, and eat it:
this is my body which will be given up for you.

Priest   When supper was ended,
    Jesus took the cup that was filled with wine.
    He thanked you, gave it to his friends, and said:

Take this, all of you, and drink from it:
 this is the cup of my blood,
the blood of the new and everlasting covenant.
It will be shed for you and for all
so that sins may be forgiven.
Then he said to them:
do this in memory of me.

We remember Jesus' death and resurrection

We do now what Jesus told us to do.
We remember his death and his resurrection
and we offer you, Father, the bread that gives us life,
and the cup that saves us.
Jesus brings us to you;
welcome us as you welcome him.

The priest invites us to renew our faith in the mystery of Christ's death, resurrection and the coming again

Let us proclaim our faith:

People 1 **Christ has died,**
Christ is risen,
Christ will come again.

2 **Dying you destroyed our death,**
rising you restored our life.
Lord Jesus, come in glory.

3 **When we eat this bread and drink this**
cup,
we proclaim your death, Lord Jesus,
until you come in glory.

4 **Lord, by your cross and resurrection**
you have set us free.
You are the Savior of the world.

We pray for all, both living and dead

Priest Father,
because you love us,
you invite us to come to your table.
Fill us with the joy of the Holy Spirit
as we receive the body and blood of your Son.

Lord,
you never forget any of your children.
We ask you to take care of those we love,
especially of N. and N.,
and we pray for those who have died.

Remember everyone who is suffering from pain or
   sorrow.
Remember Christians everywhere
and all other people in the world.

We are filled with wonder and praise
when we see what you do for us
through Jesus your Son,
and so we sing (say):

We give solemn praise and glory to God

Through him,
with him,
in him,
in the unity of the Holy Spirit,
all glory and honor is yours,
almighty Father,
for ever and ever.
All   **Amen.**

Eucharistic Prayer for Children II

We praise and thank God for the beautiful things in our life

Priest   The Lord be with you.
People   **And also with you.**
Priest   Lift up your hearts.
People   **We lift them up to the Lord.**
Priest   Let us give thanks to the Lord our God.
People   **It is right to give him thanks and praise.**
Priest   God our loving Father,
we are glad to give you thanks and praise
because you love us.
With Jesus we sing your praise:

All   **Glory to God in the highest.**
    or
    Hosanna in the highest.

Priest   Because you love us,
you gave us this great and beautiful world.
with Jesus we sing your praise:

All   **Glory to God in the highest.**
    or
    Hosanna in the highest.

Priest   Because you love us,
you sent Jesus your Son
to bring us to you
and to gather us around him
as the children of one family.
With Jesus we sing your praise:

All   **Glory to God in the highest.**

or

Hosanna in the highest.

Priest For such great love
we thank you with the angels and saints
as they praise you and sing (say):

All **Holy, holy, holy Lord, God of power and might,**
heaven and earth are full of your glory.
Hosanna in the highest.
Blessed is he who comes in the name of the Lord.
Hosanna in the highest.

Priest Blessed be Jesus, whom you sent
to be the friend of children and of the poor.
He came to show us
how we can love you, Father,
by loving one another.
He came to take away sin,
which keeps us from being friends,
and hate, which makes us all unhappy.

He promised to send the Holy Spirit,
to be with us always
so that we can live as your children.

All **Blessed is he who comes in the name of the Lord.**
Hosanna in the highest.

We ask God to let the Holy Spirit bless us

Priest God our Father,
we now ask you
to send your Holy Spirit
to change these gifts of bread and wine
into the body and blood
of Jesus Christ, our Lord.

The night before he died,
Jesus your Son showed us how much you love us.
When he was at supper with his disciples,
he took bread,
and gave you thanks and praise.
Then he broke the bread,
gave it to his friends, and said:

Take this, all of you, and eat it:
this is my body which will be given up for you.

All **Jesus has given his life for us.**

Priest When supper was ended,
Jesus took the cup that was filled with wine.
He thanked you, gave it to his friends, and said:

Take this, all of you, and drink from it:
this is the cup of my blood,
the blood of the new and everlasting covenant.
It will be shed for you and for all
so that sins may be forgiven.

All **Jesus has given his life for us.**

Priest   Then he said to them:

Do this in memory of me.

We remember Jesus' death and resurection

Priest   And so, loving Father,
we remember that Jesus died and rose again
to save the world.
He put himself into our hands,
to be the sacrifice we offer you.

All   **We praise you, we bless you, we thank you.**

We pray for the Church

Priest   Lord our God,
listen to our prayer.
Send the Holy Spirit
to all of us who share in this meal.
May this Spirit bring us closer together
in the family of the Church,
with N., our pope,
N., our bishop,
all other bishops,
and all who serve your people.

All   **We praise you, we bless you, we thank you.**

We pray for all

Priest   Remember, Father, our families and friends,
and all those we do not love as we should.

Remember those who have died.
Bring them home to you
to be with you for ever.

All **We praise you, we bless you, we thank you.**

Priest Gather us all together into your kingdom.
There we shall be happy for ever
with the Virgin Mary, Mother of God and our
mother.
There all the friends
of Jesus the Lord
will sing a song of joy.

All **We praise you, we bless you, we thank you.**

We give solemn praise and glory to God

Priest Through him,
with him,
in him,
in the unity of the Holy Spirit,
all glory and honor is yours,
almighty Father,
for ever and ever.

All **Amen.**

Eucharistic Prayer for Children III

We praise and thank God for the beautiful things in our life

Priest   The Lord be with you.
People   **And also with you.**
Priest   Lift up your hearts.
People   **We lift them up to the Lord.**
Priest   Let us give thanks to the Lord our God.
People   **It is right to give him thanks and praise.**
Priest   We thank you,
God our Father.

OUTSIDE THE EASTER SEASON
You made us to live for you and for each other.
We can see and speak to one another,
and become friends,
and share our joys and sorrows.

IN THE EASTER SEASON
You are the living God;
you have called us to share in your life,
and to be happy with you for ever.
You raised up Jesus, your Son,
the first among us to rise from the dead,
and gave him new life.
You have promised to give us new life also,
a life that will never end,
a life with no more anxiety and suffering.

Priest   And so, Father, we gladly thank you
with every one who believes in you;
with the saints and the angels,
we rejoice and praise you, saying:

We praise God

All   **Holy, holy, holy Lord, God of power and
might,
heaven and earth are full of your glory.
Hosanna in the highest.
Blessed is he who comes in the name of the Lord.
Hosanna in the highest.**

Priest   Yes, Lord, you are holy;
you are kind to us and to all.
For this we thank you.
We thank you above all for your Son, Jesus Christ.

OUTSIDE THE EASTER SEASON
You sent him into this world
because people had turned away from you
and no longer loved each other.
He opened our eyes and our hearts
to understand that we are brothers and sisters
and that you are Father of us all.

IN THE EASTER SEASON
He brought us the good news
of life to be lived with you for ever in heaven.

He showed us the way to that life,
the way of love.
He himself has gone that way before us.

He now brings us together to one table
and asks us to do what he did.

We ask God to bless our offerings

Father,
we ask you to bless these gifts of bread and wine
and make them holy.
Change them for us into the body and blood
  of Jesus Christ, your Son.

Our offerings become the body and blood of Christ

On the night before he died for us,
he had supper for the last time with his disciples.
He took bread
and gave you thanks.
He broke the bread
and gave it to his friends, saying:

Take this, all of you, and eat it:
this is my body which will be given up for you.

In the same way he took a cup of wine.
He gave you thanks
and handed the cup to his disciples, saying:

Take this, all of you, and drink from it:
this is the cup of my blood
the blood of the new and everlasting covenant.
It will be shed for you and for all
so that sins may be forgiven.

Then he said to them:

Do this in memory of me.

We remember Jesus' death and resurrection

God our Father,
we remember with joy
all that Jesus did to save us.

In this holy sacrifice,
which he gave as a gift to his Church,
we remember his death and resurrection.

Father in heaven,
accept us together with your beloved Son.
He willingly died for us,
but you raised him to life again.
We thank you and say:
All   **Glory to God in the highest.***
Priest   Jesus now lives with you in glory,
but he is also here on earth, among us.
We thank you and say:
All   **Glory to God in the highest.**
Priest   One day he will come in glory
and in his kingdom
there will be no more suffering,
no more tears, no more sadness.
We thank you and say:
All   **Glory to God in the highest.**

We pray for the family of God

Priest   Father in heaven,
you have called us
to receive the body and blood of Christ at this table
and to be filled with the joy of the Holy Spirit.

*Some other suitable words of praise may be used instead
of these.

Through this sacred meal
give us strength to please you more and more.

Lord, our God,
remember N., our pope,
N., our bishop, and all other bishops.

OUTSIDE THE EASTER SEASON
Help all who follow Jesus
to work for peace
and to bring happiness to others.

IN THE EASTER SEASON
Fill all Christians with the gladness of Easter.
Help us to bring this joy
to all who are sorrowful.

Bring us all at last
together with Mary, the Mother of God,
and all the saints,
to live with you
and to be one with Christ in heaven.

We give solemn praise and glory to God

Through him,
with him,
in him,
in the unity of the Holy Spirit,
all glory and honor is yours,
almighty Father,
for ever and ever.
All **Amen.**

PRAYERS

The Sign of the Cross
In the name of the Father,
and of the Son,
and of the Holy Spirit. Amen.

Glory to the Father
Glory to the Father, and to the Son, and to the Holy
  Spirit:
as it was in the beginning, is now, and will be forever.
  Amen.

Grace Before Meals
Bless us, O Lord, and these Your gifts
which we are about to receive
from Your bounty
through Christ our Lord. Amen.

Grace After Meals
We give You thanks, O almighty God,
for all Your benefits;
You who live and reign,
world without end. Amen.

The Hail Mary
Hail Mary, full of grace,
the Lord is with thee;
blessed art thou among women,
and blessed is the fruit
of thy womb, Jesus.
Holy Mary, Mother of God,
pray for us sinners now
and at the hour of our death. Amen.

The Our Father

Our Father, who art in heaven,
hallowed be Thy name,
Thy kingdom come,
Thy will be done,
on earth as it is in heaven.
Give us this daily bread,
and forgive us our trespasses
as we forgive those
who trespass against us,
and lead us not into temptation,
but deliver us from evil. Amen.

The Apostles' Creed

I believe in God,
the Father almighty
creator of heaven and earth.
I believe in Jesus Christ, his only Son,
our Lord. He was conceived
by the power of the Holy Spirit
and born of the Virgin Mary.
He suffered under Pontius Pilate,
was crucified, died, and was buried.
He descended to the dead.
On the third day he rose again.
He ascended into heaven,
and is seated at the right hand
of the Father.
He will come again
to judge the living and the dead.
I believe in the Holy Spirit,
the holy Catholic Church,
the communion of saints,
the forgiveness of sins,
the resurrection of the body,
and the life everlasting. Amen.

Act of Faith

O my God, I believe that you are
one God in three Divine Persons:
Father, Son and Holy Spirit.
I believe that Your Divine Son
became Man and died for our sins,
and that He will come again to
judge the living and the dead.
I believe these and all the truths
that the Catholic Church teaches,
because You have revealed them,
who can neither deceive nor
be deceived. Amen.

Act of Hope

O my God, relying on Your
almighty power and infinite mercy
and promises, I hope to obtain
pardon of my sins, the help
of Your grace and life everlasting
through the merits of Jesus Christ,
my Lord and Redeemer. Amen.

Act of Love

O my God, I love You above all things
with my whole heart and soul,
because You are all good
and worthy of all love.
I love my neighbor as myself
for the love of You.
I forgive all who have injured me
and ask pardon of all
whom I have injured. Amen.

THE REGINA PRESS
145 SHERWOOD AVENUE
FARMINGDALE, N.Y. 11735

Cover photography: Chris Sheridan

The Regina Press would like to thank Fr. Tom Tuite,
Sr. Anne Power, S.C., Principal, and all the children of
St. Aidan's Lower School, Williston Park, N.Y.

Approved for use in the dioceses of the United States of
America by the Bishops' Committee on the Liturgy.
Concordat cum originali: John A Gurrieri
Imprimatur: Edward B Clancy D.D., L.S.S.
Archbishop of Sydney
27 January, 1988

ISBN: 0-88271-166-0

Production supervised by E.J. Dwyer & Co. (Hong Kong) Ltd.
Printed in Hong Kong by Mandarin Offset